Long's Town

by Ann Rossi

illustrated by Jeff Hopkins

PEARSON

Scott
Foresman

Editorial Offices: Glenview, Illinois • Parsippany, New Jersey • New York, New York
Sales Offices: Needham, Massachusetts • Duluth, Georgia • Glenview, Illinois
Coppell, Texas • Ontario, California • Mesa, Arizona

ISBN: 0-328-13150-4

12 13 14 V0N4 14 13 12 11 10

Loni loved her town. She spent time walking and shopping with her grandma. They bought bread at the bakery and shoes at the shoe store.

From their apartment window, Loni and her grandma watched people walk and jog along the busy street. At the crosswalk, a guide dog was helping its owner cross the street.

"Grandma, I love living here. I hope our town will never change," said Loni.

"We have a great town, Loni," smiled Grandma. "But did you know that in the past, there were only farms here? It looked very different when my great-grandmother was a little girl. I'll get some pictures to show you."

Grandma showed Loni a picture of a young girl. She was standing next to a house and barn. A cow was sticking its head out of a window in the barn. Behind the girl, a field of corn stretched down to the river.

"Wow! I never knew our town used to be farmland!" exclaimed Loni as she pointed to the photo album.

"Oh my, yes," said Grandma. "My great-grandmother's family farm had cows, sheep, and goats for milk."

"They kept chickens too," continued Grandma, "but not for milk."

Loni giggled. "There's no such thing as chicken milk, Grandma! Look, your great-grandma is gathering chicken eggs in this picture."

Grandma explained that even transportation was different back then. Her great-grandmother's family traveled by boat, by horse, or on foot. There were dirt roads in the town.

"What happened to all the farms and the dirt roads?" asked Loni.

"More people settled here. Over time, farmers sold their land to builders. They built stores and schools. They paved the roads. It was a town when my grandmother was born. People moved there to find jobs," said Grandma. "This picture shows how different the town looked back then."

Grandma handed Loni another picture. "When my mother was born, cars and horses shared the road. Years later, when I was born, you never saw a horse on the street."

"Our town has changed a lot," said Loni thoughtfully. "I bet it will keep growing and changing, just like me."

Rivers and Settlements

Rivers have helped towns grow for hundreds of years. Rivers are excellent routes for transportation. Many settlers followed rivers to find new places to live. The land around a river was often good for growing crops. Rivers are a good source of water for animals and people.

Many settlements in the United States were built along rivers. Over time, these settlements grew into the large cities of the present. St. Louis, Missouri, is a city that is near the Mississippi River.

St. Louis lies along the Mississippi River.